VIKING
RETARGETING

Chapter 1:
An Intro to Retargeting

What is Retargeting?

Retargeting has come a long way in the last few years. Originally seen as a super complex and expensive tactic available only to big businesses, retargeting has recently become a must-have advertising tactic for all businesses. More importantly, it's now affordable and learnable for even the newest entrepreneur.

So what is it? Retargeting is the act of advertising to consumers based on their previous actions or behavior. Ever visited a site to learn about a certain product or brand, and suddenly you notice images of that product or brand following you all over the web? Yup, that's retargeting. And it's proven to work like a charm!

How Does it Work?

There are several types of retargeting, which we'll discuss in detail later. But the most basic form is basic site visitor retargeting and it works as follows. You take a retargeting "pixel" which is simply a bit of code that you copy and paste from your retargeting provider, and paste it on your site. From that point forward, any visitor to your site gets "cookied" as a site visitor. Your retargeting provider relies on major internet ad networks to continuously show your ad to those "cookied" visitors around the web. Essentially, rather than focusing on "cold traffic", which never converts very well, you're now focusing on bringing back "warm traffic" or repeat visitors who are already familiar with your brand and more likely to become customers.

Why Retargeting?

Retargeting has proven to be one of the most effective forms of paid advertising available. Site visitors who were retargeted via display ads are 70 percent more likely to convert on your site. The click-through rate (CTR) on display ads is a whopping 10X higher with retargeting. The results in remedying cart abandonment are impressive as well. A majority of first-time visitors are likely to abandon your checkout page and, usually, less than 10 percent of them will return later. With retargeting, you can increase the percentage of those cart "returnees" to over 25 percent! This explains why around 50 percent of all major brands have set aside specific budgets just for retargeting.

Retargeting comes in many shapes and sizes and we'll discuss the various types in the next chapter.

Types of Retargeting

There are several different types of retargeting that your business can engage in, ranging from very simple to very complex. We'll discuss some of the more popular ones below.

Site Retargeting

The most basic and easy to understand type of retargeting is site retargeting. This very simple version of retargeting simply consists of placing a retargeting pixel on your site and creating a retargeting audience out of anyone who visits it. Now that you've determined these people have an interest in, and familiarity with, your brand, you can then retarget them in the future as a "warm" audience and expect significantly better ad results than you'd experience with cold traffic.

Dynamic Retargeting

Although site retargeting can be useful and is an excellent baby step towards your retargeting goals, it doesn't present anything really custom tailored to your audience and, therefore, doesn't really utilize retargeting to its full potential. Dynamic retargeting takes things a step further by taking your traffic's specific behavior into account. Rather than just lump everyone who visits your site into one audience, dynamic retargeting reaches out to customers based on what specific products or pages they viewed. This way, you can ensure you are following users around the web with images of the specific product that they were interested in, rather than your brand in general. This makes things much more relevant for your audience and much more cost-effective for your business.

Dynamic retargeting can also be taken a few steps further. Rather than simply targeting visitors based on products they viewed, you can also target people based on whether they eventually bought the things they put in their shopping cart. This can encourage people to come back to your checkout page and finish what they started. Furthermore, targeting people based on what they DID buy allows you to advertise upsells and cross-sells that are relevant to their purchases.

Social Retargeting

Social retargeting has dominated the field for the last couple years. The concept of native advertising on Facebook and Twitter ("native" means the ads look and feel like organic content) was already incredibly powerful by itself when first introduced. Throwing retargeting into that equation simply makes it even more powerful. Social retargeting works essentially the same way as the other types of retargeting except that it's designed to target people specifically on social networks and especially in their newsfeeds/Twitter feeds. This can be done using those individual platforms' own retargeting pixels on your web properties or the pixels of another retargeting provider.

Search Retargeting

Search retargeting is a little different from the other types of retargeting in this list in that it doesn't rely on a pixel being installed on your web properties. Instead, it follows people around the web based on what keywords they previously placed into search engines. This shouldn't be confused with search engine marketing or "search advertising" which simply places ads inside the search engine results. Rather, this targets people based on their search terms, but then follows them all around the web after they leave the search engine results.

SEO Retargeting

Don't let the name fool you. SEO retargeting, unlike search retargeting, actually does depend on people landing on a "pixelled" web property. However, the key in this type of retargeting is that it tells you what search terms a person used in a search engine in order to get to your web property. The data acquired here can then be exploited in your search retargeting campaigns.

Email Retargeting

A much less talked about type of retargeting is email retargeting. This requires leveraging the retargeting systems within your email marketing platform or CRM. With email retargeting, you can retarget people across the web based on how they interact with your email campaigns. You can show a certain ad to people who opened an email but didn't click the link inside. You can show a re-engagement ad to people who haven't opened your last five emails at all. Any email behavioral patterns that may be useful to your business can be exploited with this method.

Theory is great. But understanding these tactics within the context of specific examples is even more useful. So that's what we'll be doing in the next chapter.

Chapter 3:
Retargeting Scenarios

So now that you know the basics of retargeting, it's time to look at its application within the context of several potential scenarios. We're going to have an in-depth look at some examples of advanced retargeting. Pay close attention to these, as they might prove directly relevant to your business.

The Content Hook

The content hook is a more recent development in digital marketing. It's designed to leverage the power of content marketing and to build rapport with potential customers without directly trying to sell to them. Consumers are used to the idea of businesses wanting either their money or their contact info in exchange for useful information. This frustrates them and causes all businesses to look more or less the same in their eyes. The way to stand out from the crowd and have your brand associated with positive emotions and feelings is content marketing.

Instead of sending your traffic to a lead page where you offer visitors some useful information about silver investing in exchange for an email opt-in or some other lead capture form, you send them directly to the useful content in the form of an article, blog post, or video. No signup form, no sales pitch, no nothing. Already you will have set yourself apart from your competition in an incredible way and built more goodwill associated with your brand than you can possibly imagine. Nobody else does this. The secret is, of course, that there was a retargeting pixel on that content page. Now that you've associated your brand with goodwill, you can then retarget these new raving fans with ads for your more robust silver investing report, this time asking for an email opt-in or even send them directly to a paid offer. They'll remember that you're one of the good guys (or gals) because you provided useful content without asking for anything in return. And your conversion rates will reflect this positive impression.

Cart Recovery

As mentioned earlier, cart recovery is a very popular application of retargeting. Ordinarily, when people abandon their carts or checkouts (and many, if not most, will) you can only hope for around 10 percent of them to come back and complete their purchase. With retargeting, you can increase that percentage of "returnees" by a whopping 150 percent! Here's how it might play out…

Your customer has just added your new bamboo smartphone case to their cart in your eCommerce store. Sadly, their lunch hour ends, or maybe they're convinced their spouse will nag them about spending too much. Whatever the reason, they leave the store without checking out. Lucky for you, you had a pixel installed on every page of your site. Based on the fact that they added that product to their cart but never checked out you immediately begin following them around the web with recovery ads. Everywhere they look, in the sidebar of their favorite blog, in the middle of a news article, on their Facebook newsfeed, they see an image of that bamboo phone case along with the words "you forgot something". Creepy? Maybe. Effective? Yes. It's been proven to work.

Lead Magnet Reminder

The lead magnet reminder is similar to the cart recovery scenario, but you're reminding people to grab a lead magnet if your tracking pixel indicates they never made it to your "thank you" page. Let's use the earlier example of the silver investment report. You spent a good bit of cash and effort warming up an audience with content marketing and later pitching your free but valuable report to them. For some reason they didn't type in their contact info and hit that "sign up" button. Those people who didn't make the leap will see ads all over the web with the snazzy eCover for your free report, reminding them that it's free and an immense value.

Persistent Upsell via Social

The persistent upsell is similar to the cart recovery and the lead magnet reminder scenarios. In this case, you're targeting the customers who purchased your front end offer, a video course on high-intensity interval training, but said "no thank you" to your upsell, a high-ticket home study course on fat-burning cardio routines. This time, you hit them repeatedly in their Facebook newsfeed with large 1200x628 images of your home study course bundle and a 10% discount to sweeten the deal. They'll already be familiar with the offer, they're already comfortable with buying from you in general because they bought your front-end offer, and if the price point was what made them say "no" the first time, you're now dangling a welcome 10% discount in front of them. Many of them will convert.

Webinar Reminder via Video

There's nothing new about webinar reminders. For a few years now, marketers have been using their email marketing platforms to send out reminders or follow-ups to people who registered for, but failed to attend their webinars. What is new is the video follow-up. In this scenario, let's say you've recently got 100 people to register for a webinar in which you're going to pitch a high-ticket consulting offer. 40 of these people did not show up to the webinar. In this case, rather than simply send out an email, you decide to retarget all the no-shows via Google's Youtube Ads. Your no-shows click on their favorite "funny cat fails" video only to see a short video of you popping up on screen mentioning in a chiding, good-humored tone "hey, you registered for our webinar, but you forgot to attend" and informing them of all the value they missed and why they need to catch the replay fast before you take it down. True, some people will be annoyed or creeped out by this. But the majority of them will be impressed by your very advanced and blunt use of retargeting and, if nothing else, this will build your credibility as a competent digital marketer.

JV Announcements

One less-talked-about use of advertising in general is affiliate/JV recruitment. If you're hoping to drive traffic primarily from other people's lists and simply pay them an affiliate commission for each sale they send you, you'd better be recruiting affiliates. Better-yet, you need to have a retargeting pixel on your JV/affiliate recruitment page.

Designate this audience as your JV retargeting audience and sit on it until your next product launch. In this scenario, let's say you're launching a new digital product with PLR rights. Rather than just email your old JVs and hope that a few of them notice your email amidst the sea of JV launch emails they get every day, you decide you want to invest a little bit to stand out from the crowd. You start a week-long campaign a few weeks prior to launch in which you put your JV invite ads in front of them all over the web and especially in their FB and Twitter newsfeeds. You ensure your ad has a little caption somewhere reminding them that they promoted your previous launch too. Affiliate marketers are constantly looking for launches that they can plug into their promotional calendars. That's how they make money. By standing out in this manner shortly before your launch, you drastically increase the chance of having affiliates on board and sending traffic for your next launch.

The potential applications for retargeting are endless. These were just a few scenarios that hopefully gave you a feel for how you can apply this technology in your business. Next, we'll discuss the various tools available to make these tactics accessible to your business.

Chapter 4:
Retargeting Tools

There are several platforms and suites that will allow you to leverage the retargeting strategies you've learned so far. We'll cover a few of the more popular ones right now.

AdWords

Google AdWords is arguably one of the most far-reaching platforms around. It's particularly attractive to businesses because it includes so many different advertising aspects. You can do basic search engine marketing (SEM), textual display ads and graphical banner ads all over the web, text ads on Android apps, video ads on Youtube, and so much more. Well guess what? Retargeting is right there on that list too. And what's more, retargeting is built right into all those other advertising opportunities as well as being built right into Google analytics. This makes Google AdWords an incredibly attractive option, not just for search retargeting, but for retargeting in general.

AdRoll and Perfect Audience

Retargeting platforms like AdRoll and Perfect audience are an excellent option for newcomers to retargeting. These platforms provide an SAAS suite in which users can easily track, segment, and analyze their retargeting audiences after placing a pixel on their websites. Once you're ready to start serving ads, each of these platforms have a very far-reaching display network with ad inventory all over the web as well as the option to focus on native ads inside Facebook and Twitter.

Facebook and Twitter

If you'd rather not focus on a broad display network all around the web and simply focus on native ads indie of people's social media feeds, you can always deal directly with the social networks. Facebook and Twitter each have their own retargeting platforms for advertisers to use directly. These platforms are surprisingly easy to learn and employ, even for total beginners. After copying and pasting your Facebook or Twitter retargeting pixel to your web properties, you'll be able to analyze and segment your audiences the same way you would in the previously-mentioned platforms. Then you would go through the traditional ad campaign creation process you've always used on these social platforms, but instead of creating an audience from scratch based on interests or demographics, you'd simply select your existing retargeting audience.

All of the retargeting knowledge you've gained thus far is incredibly valuable. But it'll be worth absolutely nothing if you don't apply it right now. Start leveraging the power of retargeting for your business by implementing steps of this battle plan today!

Battle Plan

Step 1: Choose one retargeting goal to focus on.

Step 2: Select the most appropriate type or retargeting for your goal.

Step 3: Choose one of the retargeting methods we covered earlier.

Step 4: Acquire an account with one of the retargeting tools above.

Step 5: Launch your first retargeting campaign.